2022

TEACHER PLANNER

Unique Design Press

Thank you for purchasing a copy of this Planner from Unique Design Press.

We create all of our books with love.

We would not be here without you. A brief review would help us alot. Please leave your feedback about this book.

This Book Belongs To:

_ _ _ _ _ _ _ _ _ _ _ _ _ _ _ _ _ _

_ _ _ _ _ _ _ _ _ _ _ _ _ _ _ _ _ _

A⁺ Teacher

DETAILS

NAME   _____

SCHOOL   _____

YEAR   _____

PHONE   _____

2022
CALENDAR

JANUARY

MO	TU	WE	TH	FR	SA	SU
					1	**2**
3	4	5	6	7	**8**	**9**
10	11	12	13	14	**15**	**16**
17	18	19	20	21	**22**	**23**
24	25	26	27	28	**29**	**30**
31						

FEBRUARY

MO	TU	WE	TH	FR	SA	SU
	1	2	3	4	**5**	**6**
7	8	9	10	11	**12**	**13**
14	15	16	17	18	**19**	**20**
21	22	23	24	25	**26**	**27**
28						

MARCH

MO	TU	WE	TH	FR	SA	SU
	1	2	3	4	**5**	**6**
7	8	9	10	11	**12**	**13**
14	15	16	17	18	**19**	**20**
21	22	23	24	25	**26**	**27**
28	29	30	31			

APRIL

MO	TU	WE	TH	FR	SA	SU
				1	**2**	**3**
4	5	6	7	8	**9**	**10**
11	12	13	14	15	**16**	**17**
18	19	20	21	22	**23**	**24**
25	26	27	28	29	**30**	

MAY

MO	TU	WE	TH	FR	SA	SU
						1
2	3	4	5	6	**7**	**8**
9	10	11	12	13	**14**	**15**
16	17	18	19	20	**21**	**22**
23	24	25	26	27	**28**	**29**
30	31					

JUNE

MO	TU	WE	TH	FR	SA	SU
		1	2	3	**4**	**5**
6	7	8	9	10	**11**	**12**
13	14	15	16	17	**18**	**19**
20	21	22	23	24	**25**	**26**
27	28	29	30			

JULY

MO	TU	WE	TH	FR	SA	SU
				1	**2**	**3**
4	5	6	7	8	**9**	**10**
11	12	13	14	15	**16**	**17**
18	19	20	21	22	**23**	**24**
25	26	27	28	29	**30**	**31**

AUGUST

MO	TU	WE	TH	FR	SA	SU
1	2	3	4	5	**6**	**7**
8	9	10	11	12	**13**	**14**
15	16	17	18	19	**20**	**21**
22	23	24	25	26	**27**	**28**
29	30	31				

SEPTEMBER

MO	TU	WE	TH	FR	SA	SU
			1	2	**3**	**4**
5	6	7	8	9	**10**	**11**
12	13	14	15	16	**17**	**18**
19	20	21	22	23	**24**	**25**
26	27	28	29	30		

OCTOBER

MO	TU	WE	TH	FR	SA	SU
					1	**2**
3	4	5	6	7	**8**	**9**
10	11	12	13	14	**15**	**16**
17	18	19	20	21	**22**	**23**
24	25	26	27	28	**29**	**30**
31						

NOVEMBER

MO	TU	WE	TH	FR	SA	SU
	1	2	3	4	**5**	**6**
7	8	9	10	11	**12**	**13**
14	15	16	17	18	**19**	**20**
21	22	23	24	25	**26**	**27**
28	29	30				

DECEMBER

MO	TU	WE	TH	FR	SA	SU
			1	2	**3**	**4**
5	6	7	8	9	**10**	**11**
12	13	14	15	16	**17**	**18**
19	20	21	22	23	**24**	**25**
26	27	28	29	30	**31**	

TIMETABLE

LESSON	M	TU	W	TH	F
1					
2					
3					
4					
5					
6					
7					
8					

January 2022

SUN	MON	TUE	WED
2	3	4	5
9	10	11	12
16	17 MARTIN LUTHER KING JR. DAY	18	19
23 / 30	24 / 31	25	26

NOTES

THU	FRI	SAT
		1 NEW YEAR'S DAY
6	7	8
13	14	15
20	21	22
27	28	29

_____

_____

_____

_____

_____

_____

_____

_____

_____

_____

_____

_____

_____

_____

_____

DECEMBER 2021

S	M	T	W	T	F	S
			1	2	3	4
5	6	7	8	9	10	11
12	13	14	15	16	17	18
19	20	21	22	23	24	25
26	27	28	29	30	31	

◇◇◇◇◇◇◇◇◇◇◇◇◇◇◇

FEBRUARY 2022

S	M	T	W	T	F	S
		1	2	3	4	5
6	7	8	9	10	11	12
13	14	15	16	17	18	19
20	21	22	23	24	25	26
27	28					

LESSON PLAN

MONDAY	TUESDAY	WEDNESDAY

THURSDAY	FRIDAY	SATURDAY

LESSON PLAN

MONDAY

TUESDAY

WEDNESDAY

THURSDAY

FRIDAY

SATURDAY

LESSON PLAN

MONDAY	TUESDAY	WEDNESDAY

THURSDAY	FRIDAY	SATURDAY

LESSON PLAN

MONDAY	TUESDAY	WEDNESDAY

THURSDAY	FRIDAY	SATURDAY

LESSON PLAN

MONDAY	TUESDAY	WEDNESDAY

THURSDAY	FRIDAY	SATURDAY

February 2022

SUN	MON	TUE	WED
		1	2 GROUNDHOG DAY
6	7	8	9
13	14 VALENTINE'S DAY	15	16
20	21 PRESIDENTS' DAY	22	23
27	28		

NOTES

THU	FRI	SAT
3	4	5
10	11	12
17	18	19
24	25	26

_____
_____
_____
_____
_____
_____
_____
_____
_____
_____
_____
_____
_____
_____
_____
_____
_____

JANUARY 2022

S	M	T	W	T	F	S
						1
2	3	4	5	6	7	8
9	10	11	12	13	14	15
16	17	18	19	20	21	22
23	24	25	26	27	28	29
30	31					

MARCH 2022

S	M	T	W	T	F	S
		1	2	3	4	5
6	7	8	9	10	11	12
13	14	15	16	17	18	19
20	21	22	23	24	25	26
27	28	29	30	31		

LESSON PLAN

MONDAY	TUESDAY	WEDNESDAY

THURSDAY	FRIDAY	SATURDAY

LESSON PLAN

MONDAY

TUESDAY

WEDNESDAY

THURSDAY

FRIDAY

SATURDAY

LESSON PLAN

MONDAY	TUESDAY	WEDNESDAY

THURSDAY	FRIDAY	SATURDAY

LESSON PLAN

MONDAY

TUESDAY

WEDNESDAY

THURSDAY

FRIDAY

SATURDAY

LESSON PLAN

MONDAY	TUESDAY	WEDNESDAY

THURSDAY	FRIDAY	SATURDAY

March 2022

SUN	MON	TUE	WED
		1	2
6	7	8	9
13	14	15	16
20	21	22	23
27	28	29	30

NOTES

THU	FRI	SAT
3	4	5
10	11	12
17	18	19
ST. PATRICK'S DAY		
24	25	26
31		

_____
_____
_____
_____
_____
_____
_____
_____
_____
_____
_____
_____
_____
_____
_____
_____

FEBRUARY 2022

S	M	T	W	T	F	S
		1	2	3	4	5
6	7	8	9	10	11	12
13	14	15	16	17	18	19
20	21	22	23	24	25	26
27	28					

◇◇◇◇◇◇◇◇◇◇◇◇◇◇◇

APRIL 2022

S	M	T	W	T	F	S
					1	2
3	4	5	6	7	8	9
10	11	12	13	14	15	16
17	18	19	20	21	22	23
24	25	26	27	28	29	30

LESSON PLAN

MONDAY	TUESDAY	WEDNESDAY

THURSDAY	FRIDAY	SATURDAY

LESSON PLAN

MONDAY	TUESDAY	WEDNESDAY

THURSDAY	FRIDAY	SATURDAY

LESSON PLAN

MONDAY	TUESDAY	WEDNESDAY

THURSDAY	FRIDAY	SATURDAY

LESSON PLAN

MONDAY	TUESDAY	WEDNESDAY

THURSDAY	FRIDAY	SATURDAY

LESSON PLAN

MONDAY

TUESDAY

WEDNESDAY

THURSDAY

FRIDAY

SATURDAY

April 2022

SUN	MON	TUE	WED
3	4	5	6
10	11	12	13
17 EASTER DAY	18 TAX DAY	19	20
24	25	26	27

NOTES

THU	FRI	SAT
	1	2
7	8	9
14	15	16
21	22	23
28	29	30

MARCH 2022

S	M	T	W	T	F	S
		1	2	3	4	5
6	7	8	9	10	11	12
13	14	15	16	17	18	19
20	21	22	23	24	25	26
27	28	29	30	31		

MAY 2022

S	M	T	W	T	F	S
1	2	3	4	5	6	7
8	9	10	11	12	13	14
15	16	17	18	19	20	21
22	23	24	25	26	27	28
29	30	31				

LESSON PLAN

MONDAY	TUESDAY	WEDNESDAY

THURSDAY	FRIDAY	SATURDAY

LESSON PLAN

MONDAY	TUESDAY	WEDNESDAY

THURSDAY	FRIDAY	SATURDAY

LESSON PLAN

MONDAY	TUESDAY	WEDNESDAY

THURSDAY	FRIDAY	SATURDAY

LESSON PLAN

MONDAY	TUESDAY	WEDNESDAY

THURSDAY	FRIDAY	SATURDAY

LESSON PLAN

MONDAY

TUESDAY

WEDNESDAY

THURSDAY

FRIDAY

SATURDAY

May 2022

SUN	MON	TUE	WED
1	2	3	4
8 MOTHER'S DAY	9	10	11
15	16	17	18
22	23	24	25
29	30 MEMORIAL DAY	31	

NOTES

THU	FRI	SAT
5	6	7
CINCO DE MAYO		
12	13	14
19	20	21
26	27	28

_____
_____
_____
_____
_____
_____
_____
_____
_____
_____
_____
_____
_____
_____
_____
_____

APRIL 2022

S	M	T	W	T	F	S
					1	2
3	4	5	6	7	8	9
10	11	12	13	14	15	16
17	18	19	20	21	22	23
24	25	26	27	28	29	30

◇◇◇◇◇◇◇◇◇◇◇◇◇◇◇

JUNE 2022

S	M	T	W	T	F	S
			1	2	3	4
5	6	7	8	9	10	11
12	13	14	15	16	17	18
19	20	21	22	23	24	25
26	27	28	29	30		

LESSON PLAN

MONDAY	TUESDAY	WEDNESDAY

THURSDAY	FRIDAY	SATURDAY

LESSON PLAN

MONDAY	TUESDAY	WEDNESDAY

THURSDAY	FRIDAY	SATURDAY

LESSON PLAN

MONDAY	TUESDAY	WEDNESDAY

THURSDAY	FRIDAY	SATURDAY

LESSON PLAN

MONDAY	TUESDAY	WEDNESDAY

THURSDAY	FRIDAY	SATURDAY

LESSON PLAN

MONDAY	TUESDAY	WEDNESDAY

THURSDAY	FRIDAY	SATURDAY

June 2022

SUN	MON	TUE	WED
			1
5	6	7	8
12	13	14	15
19 FATHER'S DAY	20	21	22
26	27	28	29

NOTES

THU	FRI	SAT
2	3	4
9	10	11
16	17	18
23	24	25
30		

MAY 2022

S	M	T	W	T	F	S
1	2	3	4	5	6	7
8	9	10	11	12	13	14
15	16	17	18	19	20	21
22	23	24	25	26	27	28
29	30	31				

JULY 2022

S	M	T	W	T	F	S
					1	2
3	4	5	6	7	8	9
10	11	12	13	14	15	16
17	18	19	20	21	22	23
24	25	26	27	28	29	30
31						

LESSON PLAN

MONDAY	TUESDAY	WEDNESDAY

THURSDAY	FRIDAY	SATURDAY

LESSON PLAN

MONDAY	TUESDAY	WEDNESDAY

THURSDAY	FRIDAY	SATURDAY

LESSON PLAN

MONDAY	TUESDAY	WEDNESDAY

THURSDAY	FRIDAY	SATURDAY

LESSON PLAN

MONDAY	TUESDAY	WEDNESDAY

THURSDAY	FRIDAY	SATURDAY

LESSON PLAN

MONDAY	TUESDAY	WEDNESDAY

THURSDAY	FRIDAY	SATURDAY

July 2022

SUN	MON	TUE	WED
3	4 INDEPENDENCE DAY	5	6
10	11	12	13
17	18	19	20
24 31	25	26	27

NOTES

THU	FRI	SAT
	1	2
7	8	9
14	15	16
21	22	23
28	29	30

_____
_____
_____
_____
_____
_____
_____
_____
_____
_____
_____
_____
_____
_____
_____
_____

JUNE 2022

S	M	T	W	T	F	S
			1	2	3	4
5	6	7	8	9	10	11
12	13	14	15	16	17	18
19	20	21	22	23	24	25
26	27	28	29	30		

AUGUST 2022

S	M	T	W	T	F	S
	1	2	3	4	5	6
7	8	9	10	11	12	13
14	15	16	17	18	19	20
21	22	23	24	25	26	27
28	29	30	31			

LESSON PLAN

MONDAY	TUESDAY	WEDNESDAY

THURSDAY	FRIDAY	SATURDAY

LESSON PLAN

MONDAY	TUESDAY	WEDNESDAY

THURSDAY	FRIDAY	SATURDAY

LESSON PLAN

MONDAY	TUESDAY	WEDNESDAY

THURSDAY	FRIDAY	SATURDAY

LESSON PLAN

MONDAY	TUESDAY	WEDNESDAY

THURSDAY	FRIDAY	SATURDAY

LESSON PLAN

MONDAY	TUESDAY	WEDNESDAY

THURSDAY	FRIDAY	SATURDAY

August 2022

SUN	MON	TUE	WED
	1	2	3
7	8	9	10
14	15	16	17
21	22	23	24
28	29	30	31

NOTES

THU	FRI	SAT
4	5	6
11	12	13
18	19	20
25	26	27

_____
_____
_____
_____
_____
_____
_____
_____
_____
_____
_____
_____
_____
_____
_____

JULY 2022

S	M	T	W	T	F	S
					1	2
3	4	5	6	7	8	9
10	11	12	13	14	15	16
17	18	19	20	21	22	23
24	25	26	27	28	29	30
31						

◇◇◇◇◇◇◇◇◇◇◇◇◇◇

SEPTEMBER 2022

S	M	T	W	T	F	S
				1	2	3
4	5	6	7	8	9	10
11	12	13	14	15	16	17
18	19	20	21	22	23	24
25	26	27	28	29	30	

LESSON PLAN

MONDAY

TUESDAY

WEDNESDAY

THURSDAY

FRIDAY

SATURDAY

LESSON PLAN

MONDAY

TUESDAY

WEDNESDAY

THURSDAY

FRIDAY

SATURDAY

LESSON PLAN

MONDAY	TUESDAY	WEDNESDAY

THURSDAY	FRIDAY	SATURDAY

LESSON PLAN

MONDAY

TUESDAY

WEDNESDAY

THURSDAY

FRIDAY

SATURDAY

LESSON PLAN

MONDAY	TUESDAY	WEDNESDAY

THURSDAY	FRIDAY	SATURDAY

September 2022

SUN	MON	TUE	WED
4	5	6	7
	LABOR DAY		
11	12	13	14
18	19	20	21
25	26	27	28

NOTES

THU	FRI	SAT
1	2	3
8	9	10
15	16	17
22	23	24
29	30	

_____
_____
_____
_____
_____
_____
_____
_____
_____
_____
_____
_____
_____
_____

AUGUST 2022

S	M	T	W	T	F	S
	1	2	3	4	5	6
7	8	9	10	11	12	13
14	15	16	17	18	19	20
21	22	23	24	25	26	27
28	29	30	31			

◇◇◇◇◇◇◇◇◇◇◇◇◇◇◇

OCTOBER 2022

S	M	T	W	T	F	S
						1
2	3	4	5	6	7	8
9	10	11	12	13	14	15
16	17	18	19	20	21	22
23	24	25	26	27	28	29
30	31					

LESSON PLAN

MONDAY	TUESDAY	WEDNESDAY

THURSDAY	FRIDAY	SATURDAY

LESSON PLAN

MONDAY	TUESDAY	WEDNESDAY

THURSDAY	FRIDAY	SATURDAY

LESSON PLAN

MONDAY

TUESDAY

WEDNESDAY

THURSDAY

FRIDAY

SATURDAY

LESSON PLAN

MONDAY	TUESDAY	WEDNESDAY

THURSDAY	FRIDAY	SATURDAY

LESSON PLAN

MONDAY	TUESDAY	WEDNESDAY

THURSDAY	FRIDAY	SATURDAY

October 2022

SUN	MON	TUE	WED
2	3	4	5
9	10 COLUMBUS DAY	11	12
16	17	18	19
23 / 30	24 / 31 HALLOWEEN	25	26

Verse/Quote_____

NOTES

THU	FRI	SAT
		1
6	7	8
13	14	15
20	21	22
27	28	29

_____
_____
_____
_____
_____
_____
_____
_____
_____
_____
_____
_____
_____
_____
_____
_____
_____

SEPTEMBER 2022

S	M	T	W	T	F	S
				1	2	3
4	5	6	7	8	9	10
11	12	13	14	15	16	17
18	19	20	21	22	23	24
25	26	27	28	29	30	

NOVEMBER 2022

S	M	T	W	T	F	S
		1	2	3	4	5
6	7	8	9	10	11	12
13	14	15	16	17	18	19
20	21	22	23	24	25	26
27	28	29	30			

LESSON PLAN

MONDAY	TUESDAY	WEDNESDAY

THURSDAY	FRIDAY	SATURDAY

LESSON PLAN

MONDAY	TUESDAY	WEDNESDAY

THURSDAY	FRIDAY	SATURDAY

LESSON PLAN

MONDAY	TUESDAY	WEDNESDAY

THURSDAY	FRIDAY	SATURDAY

LESSON PLAN

MONDAY	TUESDAY	WEDNESDAY

THURSDAY	FRIDAY	SATURDAY

LESSON PLAN

MONDAY	TUESDAY	WEDNESDAY

THURSDAY	FRIDAY	SATURDAY

November 2022

SUN	MON	TUE	WED
		1	2
6	7	8 ELECTION DAY	9
13	14	15	16
20	21	22	23
27	28	29	30

NOTES

THU	FRI	SAT
3	4	5
10	11	12
	VETERAN'S DAY	
17	18	19
24	25	26
THANKSGIVING DAY	BLACK FRIDAY	

_____
_____
_____
_____
_____
_____
_____
_____
_____
_____
_____
_____
_____
_____
_____
_____

OCTOBER 2022

S	M	T	W	T	F	S
						1
2	3	4	5	6	7	8
9	10	11	12	13	14	15
16	17	18	19	20	21	22
23	24	25	26	27	28	29
30	31					

◇◇◇◇◇◇◇◇◇◇◇◇◇◇

DECEMBER 2022

S	M	T	W	T	F	S
				1	2	3
4	5	6	7	8	9	10
11	12	13	14	15	16	17
18	19	20	21	22	23	24
25	26	27	28	29	30	31

LESSON PLAN

MONDAY	TUESDAY	WEDNESDAY

THURSDAY	FRIDAY	SATURDAY

LESSON PLAN

MONDAY	TUESDAY	WEDNESDAY

THURSDAY	FRIDAY	SATURDAY

LESSON PLAN

MONDAY	TUESDAY	WEDNESDAY

THURSDAY	FRIDAY	SATURDAY

LESSON PLAN

MONDAY	TUESDAY	WEDNESDAY

THURSDAY	FRIDAY	SATURDAY

LESSON PLAN

MONDAY	TUESDAY	WEDNESDAY

THURSDAY	FRIDAY	SATURDAY

December 2022

SUN	MON	TUE	WED
4	5	6	7
11	12	13	14
18	19	20	21
25	26	27	28

CHRISTMAS DAY

NOTES

THU	FRI	SAT
1	2	3
8	9	10
15	16	17
22	23	24
		CHRISTMAS EVE
29	30	31
		NEW YEAR'S EVE

_____
_____
_____
_____
_____
_____
_____
_____
_____
_____
_____
_____
_____
_____
_____
_____
_____
_____

NOVEMBER 2022

S	M	T	W	T	F	S
		1	2	3	4	5
6	7	8	9	10	11	12
13	14	15	16	17	18	19
20	21	22	23	24	25	26
27	28	29	30			

JANUARY 2023

S	M	T	W	T	F	S
1	2	3	4	5	6	7
8	9	10	11	12	13	14
15	16	17	18	19	20	21
22	23	24	25	26	27	28
29	30	31				

LESSON PLAN

MONDAY	TUESDAY	WEDNESDAY

THURSDAY	FRIDAY	SATURDAY

LESSON PLAN

MONDAY	TUESDAY	WEDNESDAY

THURSDAY	FRIDAY	SATURDAY

LESSON PLAN

MONDAY	TUESDAY	WEDNESDAY

THURSDAY	FRIDAY	SATURDAY

LESSON PLAN

MONDAY	TUESDAY	WEDNESDAY

THURSDAY	FRIDAY	SATURDAY

LESSON PLAN

MONDAY	TUESDAY	WEDNESDAY

THURSDAY	FRIDAY	SATURDAY

Students CONTACT List

Class

ROLL	Phone Or Email	Name
--------	----------------------------------	--
--------	----------------------------------	--
--------	----------------------------------	--
--------	----------------------------------	--
--------	----------------------------------	--
--------	----------------------------------	--
--------	----------------------------------	--
--------	----------------------------------	--
--------	----------------------------------	--
--------	----------------------------------	--
--------	----------------------------------	--
--------	----------------------------------	--
--------	----------------------------------	--
--------	----------------------------------	--

Notes : --

Teacher CONTACT List

Class --

ROLL	Phone Or Email	Name
--------	------------------------------	--
--------	------------------------------	--
--------	------------------------------	--
--------	------------------------------	--
--------	------------------------------	--
--------	------------------------------	--
--------	------------------------------	--
--------	------------------------------	--
--------	------------------------------	--
--------	------------------------------	--
--------	------------------------------	--
--------	------------------------------	--
--------	------------------------------	--
--------	------------------------------	--

Notes : --

ASSESSMENT

SUBJECT													
STUDENT													

ASSESSMENT

SUBJECT													
STUDENT													

MY GOALS

SHORT TERM: PERSONAL

_____

_____

_____

SHORT TERM: PROFESSIONAL

_____

_____

_____

LONG TERM: PERSONAL

_____

_____

_____

LONG TERM: PROFESSIONAL

_____

_____

_____

NOTES

NOTES

Printed in Great Britain
by Amazon